The Flourishing Advantage
STUDY GUIDE

Copyright © 2024 by Dr. Wayne Hammond

Published by AVAIL

All rights reserved. No portion of this book may be reproduced, stored in a retrieval system, or transmitted in any form or by any means—electronic, mechanical, photocopy, recording, scanning, or other—except for brief quotations in critical reviews or articles, without prior written permission of the author.

For foreign and subsidiary rights, contact the author.

Cover design by Sara Young
Cover photo by ARGUS PHOTOGRAPHER
Author photo on cover Andrew van Tilborgh

ISBN: 978-1-962401-22-7   1 2 3 4 5 6 7 8 9 10

Printed in the United States of America

The Flourishing Advantage
STUDY GUIDE

Dr. Wayne Hammond

AVAIL

CONTENTS

CHAPTER 1. Inside Out 6

CHAPTER 2. Beyond Resilience 12

CHAPTER 3. Three Pillars 18

CHAPTER 4. All in Your Head 24

CHAPTER 5. Connect 30

CHAPTER 6. Inspire 34

CHAPTER 7. Build 40

CHAPTER 8. Empower 46

CHAPTER 9. The Journey 52

CHAPTER 10. Flourishing at Home 58

CHAPTER 11. Flourishing at Work 64

CHAPTER 12. Unleash Your Potential! 70

The Flourishing Advantage

A Mindset Shift from Surviving to Thriving

Dr. Wayne Hammond

CHAPTER 1

Inside Out

*With a foundation of confidence and hope,
we can handle virtually anything.*

READING TIME

As you read Chapter 1: "Inside Out" in *The Flourishing Advantage*, review, reflect on, and respond to the text by answering the following questions.

REVIEW, REFLECT, AND RESPOND

What is the central tension described in this chapter, and how does it affect human behavior and motivation?

_____
_____
_____
_____
_____
_____
_____
_____
_____
_____
_____

What are the implicit promises of success, pleasure, and approval? Why are they inadequate foundations for flourishing?

_____
_____
_____
_____
_____
_____
_____
_____
_____
_____

Define the concept of "flourishing" as presented in this chapter. How does it differ from conventional notions of success?

_____
_____
_____
_____
_____
_____
_____
_____
_____
_____
_____

Discuss the importance of strength-based support and active listening in facilitating personal growth and empowerment.

_____
_____
_____
_____
_____
_____
_____
_____
_____
_____
_____
_____

Explain the significance of embracing an inside-out approach to personal development. How does this approach differ from seeking external validation?

_____
_____
_____
_____
_____
_____
_____
_____
_____
_____
_____

Do you know anyone who lives with inside-out motivation? What is true of that person's purpose, confidence, and relationships?

_____
_____
_____
_____
_____
_____
_____
_____
_____
_____
_____

Reflect on the role of relationships in promoting flourishing. Why are supportive connections essential for personal growth and resilience?

___

Take some time to write elements of your life's story on a timeline. Be as detailed as you want to be.

___

What emotions resurfaced as you recalled pleasant and painful experiences?

_____
_____
_____
_____
_____
_____

Do you believe your story holds the key to a genuinely meaningful and flourishing life? Why or why not?

_____
_____
_____
_____
_____
_____

What do you hope to get out of this book?

_____
_____
_____
_____
_____
_____

CHAPTER 2
Beyond Resilience

Resilience is bouncing back from adversity, but flourishing is bouncing forward to new opportunities.

READING TIME

As you read Chapter 2: "Beyond Resilience" in *The Flourishing Advantage*, review, reflect on, and respond to the text by answering the following questions.

REVIEW, REFLECT, AND RESPOND

Define resilience and flourishing. How do these concepts differ, and what are the key elements of each?

_____
_____
_____
_____
_____
_____
_____
_____
_____
_____

What are some reasons why getting back to baseline seems good enough? Why isn't it?

_____
_____
_____
_____
_____
_____
_____
_____
_____
_____

How might you have responded if you were a student and a new teacher taught your class "How to Fail"?

_____
_____
_____
_____
_____
_____
_____
_____
_____
_____

Discuss the significance of a paradigm shift in psychology from focusing on deficits to emphasizing strengths and positive qualities.

_____
_____
_____
_____
_____
_____
_____
_____
_____
_____

Explain the four phases of transformational change: Connect, Inspire, Build, Empower. How do these phases contribute to personal growth and flourishing?

_____
_____
_____
_____
_____
_____
_____
_____
_____
_____
_____

Describe the characteristics of individuals who flourish. How do these characteristics contribute to overall well-being and fulfillment?

_____
_____
_____
_____
_____
_____
_____
_____
_____
_____
_____

Reflect on the importance of emotional intelligence and self-awareness in fostering resilience and promoting flourishing.

_____
_____
_____
_____
_____
_____
_____
_____
_____
_____
_____

How would you rate the quality of your connection with at least one person who believes in you?

_____
_____
_____
_____
_____
_____
_____
_____
_____
_____
_____

How free do you feel to be inspired to do something creative and new? How well are you building a reservoir of knowledge and skills? How empowered do you feel to be all you can be?

_____
_____
_____
_____
_____
_____
_____
_____
_____
_____
_____
_____
_____
_____
_____
_____
_____
_____
_____
_____

CHAPTER 3

Three Pillars

A flourishing life rests on three pillars: personal strengths of self-awareness and self-confidence, environmental strengths of supportive connections, and the acquisition of performance strengths through repeated courageous experiences.

READING TIME

As you read Chapter 3: "Three Pillars" in *The Flourishing Advantage*, rreview, reflect on, and respond to the text by answering the following questions.

REVIEW, REFLECT, AND RESPOND

What are the three pillars essential for a flourishing life, and how do they interact with each other?

_____
_____
_____
_____
_____
_____
_____
_____
_____
_____

What are some ways people acquire self-awareness and self-confidence?

_____
_____
_____
_____
_____
_____
_____
_____
_____
_____

On a scale of 0 (not at all) to 10 (fully), rate your level of personal strength. Explain your answer.

    1   2   3   4   5   6   7   8   9   10

_____
_____
_____
_____
_____
_____
_____
_____
_____

Environmental strengths are life-giving relationships—at home, at work, and everywhere we connect with people. On a scale of 0 (not at all) to 10 (fully), rate your level of environmental strength. Explain your answer.

    1   2   3   4   5   6   7   8   9   10

_____
_____
_____
_____
_____
_____
_____
_____
_____

Describe the significance of supportive relationships in the context of environmental strengths. How do these relationships contribute to personal growth and resilience?

_____
_____
_____
_____
_____
_____
_____
_____
_____
_____

How would you identify and describe your performance strengths?

_____
_____
_____
_____
_____
_____
_____
_____
_____
_____
_____
_____
_____

On a scale of 0 (not at all) to 10 (fully), rate your level of these strengths. Explain your answer.

1 2 3 4 5 6 7 8 9 10

_____
_____
_____
_____
_____
_____
_____
_____
_____

Why does the "brain on a stick" educational system (in schools, in training employees, and at home) not work very well?

_____
_____
_____
_____
_____
_____
_____
_____
_____
_____
_____
_____

How can we address the past so we can get beyond it and focus on today?

_____
_____
_____
_____
_____
_____
_____
_____
_____
_____

How would you describe the "incarnational model," in which counselors, teachers, coaches, mentors, and parents focus on connecting and inspiring those with whom they have relationships?

_____
_____
_____
_____
_____
_____
_____
_____
_____
_____

CHAPTER 4

All in Your Head

*We may assume we can't change
. . . we're wrong. Our brains are
wonderfully constructed to change.*

READING TIME

As you read Chapter 4: "All in Your Head" in *The Flourishing Advantage*, review, reflect on, and respond to the text by answering the following questions.

REVIEW, REFLECT, AND RESPOND

How would you describe the feelings, motivations, attitudes, and behaviors of people who have each of the four mindsets?

1) Surviving:_____
_____
_____
_____
_____
_____

2) Protecting:_____
_____
_____
_____
_____
_____

3) Striving:_____
_____
_____
_____
_____
_____

4) Thriving:_____
_____
_____
_____
_____
_____

How do the above mindsets influence one's approach to challenges and opportunities?

___

According to Carol Dweck's research, what is the key factor that determines success in life, and how does it differ from traditional measures like background, education, intelligence, or talent?

___

Draw a timeline of your life, from birth to today. Note the significant blocks of time: childhood, high school, higher education, early years of career and marriage, children, job changes, moves, etc. Which of the four mindsets did you have in each of those blocks of time?

_____
_____
_____
_____
_____
_____
_____
_____
_____
_____

What is the evidence of the mindsets in each period?

_____
_____
_____
_____
_____
_____
_____
_____
_____
_____
_____
_____

Explain the role of the amygdala and hippocampus in the brain's response to stress, emotional regulation, memory formation, and learning processes. How do these brain regions contribute to the development of different mindsets?

_____
_____
_____
_____
_____
_____
_____
_____
_____
_____
_____

Does the concept of neuroplasticity give you hope for real transformation? Explain your answer.

_____
_____
_____
_____
_____
_____
_____
_____
_____
_____
_____

How do positive experiences and social connections impact brain function and structure, particularly in relation to the release of neurotransmitters like dopamine and oxytocin? Provide examples of activities or interventions that promote positive brain changes.

What difference does it make (or will it make) for you to realize that reading and talking aren't enough to promote genuine change, and what works is a new pattern of courageous, lived experiences?

CHAPTER 5

Connect

The obsession with our deficiencies continues until we form the kind of affirming connections we've needed all of our lives. And it's never too late to find and form these connections.

READING TIME

As you read Chapter 5: "Connect" in *The Flourishing Advantage*, review, reflect on, and respond to the text by answering the following questions.

REVIEW, REFLECT, AND RESPOND

What are some signs someone is in surviving mode?

_____
_____
_____
_____
_____
_____
_____
_____
_____
_____

How would you characterize the relationships of someone in survival mode?

_____
_____
_____
_____
_____
_____
_____
_____
_____
_____
_____

Explain how the lack of meaningful connections with others affects one's self-perception and behavior?

_____
_____
_____
_____
_____
_____

Who has been the person who has connected with you most powerfully and positively? Describe the person's impact on you.

_____
_____
_____
_____
_____
_____

Which attachment style best describes your childhood? Explain your answer.

_____
_____
_____
_____
_____
_____

How has that style shown up in your life as an adult?

Describe the four attachment styles identified by John Bowlby and their implications for personal relationships and self-perception.

The action points at the end of the chapter are "identify the need," "engage," and "stay connected." Look at those sections and write a plan for finding and benefitting from being connected with a supportive person.

CHAPTER 6

Inspire

Connection answers the who question; inspiration points you to the what, why, and how.

READING TIME

As you read Chapter 6: "Inspire" in *The Flourishing Advantage*, review, reflect on, and respond to the text by answering the following questions.

REVIEW, REFLECT, AND RESPOND

What are some reasons it's important to trust someone and feel valued so you can receive that person's inspiring messages? What happens to those messages if we don't trust the person?

_____
_____
_____
_____
_____
_____
_____
_____

How would you describe the reasons connecting and inspiring are the cornerstones of growth?

_____
_____
_____
_____
_____
_____
_____
_____

What is the relationship between trust and inspiration in personal growth and development?

_____
_____
_____
_____
_____
_____
_____
_____
_____
_____

As you've read this chapter, what opportunities have come to mind, maybe those you missed in the past?

_____
_____
_____
_____
_____
_____
_____
_____
_____
_____

What are the fears that keep people imprisoned in passivity? How did the fears rob them of initiative?

_____
_____
_____
_____
_____
_____
_____
_____
_____
_____
_____

What role does faith play in responding to inspirational messages and overcoming personal barriers?

_____
_____
_____
_____
_____
_____
_____
_____
_____
_____
_____

Answer the questions under "Becoming a Candidate for Inspiration."

What are the steps you want and need to take?

How will you prepare to take them?

When and how will you take them?

How will you process your experiences?

CHAPTER 7

Build

A foundation of connecting and inspiring is essential for us to utilize our strengths in constructive ways in the building phase.

READING TIME

As you read Chapter 7: "Build" in *The Flourishing Advantage*, review, reflect on, and respond to the text by answering the following questions.

REVIEW, REFLECT, AND RESPOND

Can you recall a time when someone was intensely for you, like a football coach cheering his quarterback on at a crucial point in a game? If so, how did it make you feel? If not, what do you think you've missed?

_____
_____
_____
_____
_____
_____
_____
_____
_____

What is the difference between validation and affirmation?

_____
_____
_____
_____
_____
_____
_____
_____
_____
_____
_____

Describe the difference in the impact of being praised for your effort and your tenacity to stay in the process instead of your intelligence and skill.

___

What can you say to a family member or teammate besides, "Good job"?

What difference do you think doing the above will make?

_____

What has to happen in your mind for this change to become a habit?

_____

How do small wins (and good lessons from failures) affect our brains?

_____
_____
_____
_____
_____
_____
_____
_____
_____
_____
_____

Review the section on nagging fears and answer the questions.

_____
_____
_____
_____
_____
_____
_____
_____
_____
_____
_____
_____

In what ways do fears, both rational and irrational, play a role in the building phase of transformation, and how can individuals address these fears to continue progressing?

_____
_____
_____
_____
_____
_____
_____
_____
_____
_____

Which of the stories about overcoming is most meaningful to you? Explain your answer.

_____
_____
_____
_____
_____
_____
_____
_____
_____
_____

CHAPTER 8

Empower

People who feel empowered are fully present in the moment—their confidence has overcome any tendency to manipulate or dominate people out of fear.

READING TIME

As you read Chapter 8: "Empower" in *The Flourishing Advantage*, review, reflect on, and respond to the text by answering the following questions.

REVIEW, REFLECT, AND RESPOND

Describe the journey of empowerment as outlined in this chapter. How do individuals progress through the stages of surviving, protecting, striving, and thriving?

_____
_____
_____
_____
_____
_____
_____
_____
_____

What traits may a person need to build before the empowerment stage?

_____
_____
_____
_____
_____
_____
_____
_____
_____
_____

Why is being curious a characteristic of someone who feels empowered?

What may have inhibited curiosity before? What unleashes it now? And humility? Boldness?

In this chapter, I mentioned that some people have a certain "spark" of purpose and passion. Can someone have that spark in the stages of surviving and protecting? Why or why not?

_____
_____
_____
_____
_____
_____
_____
_____
_____
_____

Can they have the spark in the building stage? Why or why not?

_____
_____
_____
_____
_____
_____
_____
_____
_____
_____
_____

Discuss the importance of humility in empowerment. How does humility differ from pride, and why is it essential for fostering genuine empowerment?

_____
_____
_____
_____
_____
_____
_____
_____
_____
_____
_____

What is most attractive to you about the description in this chapter of being empowered?

_____
_____
_____
_____
_____
_____
_____
_____
_____
_____
_____
_____

Do you feel any sense of resistance? If so, describe it.

Compare and contrast the attitudes of dependence and empowerment as exemplified in the conversation between two young people entering the workforce. What traits distinguish an empowered individual from one who relies heavily on others for decision-making?

CHAPTER 9

The Journey

*To get on the right path and move forward,
we need to understand the process.*

READING TIME

As you read Chapter 9: "The Journey" in *The Flourishing Advantage*, review, reflect on, and respond to the text by answering the following questions.

REVIEW, REFLECT, AND RESPOND

How do you think the modern conveniences of an "instant society" have shaped your expectations of personal growth?

_____
_____
_____
_____
_____
_____
_____
_____
_____

What is the combined impact on our journey of insight and grace? Why do we need both?

_____
_____
_____
_____
_____
_____
_____
_____
_____
_____
_____

Discuss the resistance to change, including common fears that hinder individuals from embarking on a journey of growth.

_____
_____
_____
_____
_____
_____
_____
_____
_____
_____

As you learn about this process of growth, what are some specific assumptions you need to unlearn? What difference will it make?

_____
_____
_____
_____
_____
_____
_____
_____
_____
_____
_____

Why is it important to keep relearning the concepts of truth and grace?

How does the metaphor of holding up a string illustrate the importance of accumulating courage and confidence over time in the face of challenges?

How would you describe the importance of being understood? What happens when you feel deeply known and valued? What happens when you don't?

Which of the signs of progress are you seeing (or beginning to see) in yourself?

What's your next step on the journey?

CHAPTER 10

Flourishing at Home

We can take the principles and perspectives of a flourishing life into our most important relationships. The people who live under our roofs are in our inner circle ... or they should be ... and they can be.

READING TIME

As you read Chapter 10: "Flourishing at Home" in *The Flourishing Advantage*, review, reflect on, and respond to the text by answering the following questions.

REVIEW, REFLECT, AND RESPOND

According to this chapter, what is the primary message that spouses and children long to hear and feel deep in their hearts?

_____
_____
_____
_____
_____
_____
_____
_____
_____

How would you describe the changing role of parents as kids grow from infancy to childhood to adolescence to become young adults?

_____
_____
_____
_____
_____
_____
_____
_____
_____
_____

Why do people often default to high control in their most important relationships? What underlying emotion drives this behavior?

___

What are some key principles of strengths-based parenting, and how do they differ from traditional parenting approaches?

___

At which stage of your children's development do (or did) you feel most comfortable? Which one feels most uncomfortable? Explain your answer.

If you have children or grandchildren, what are some concrete ways you can connect with, inspire, build, and empower each of them?

Look back at the strategies of strengths-based parenting. Which of the nine are you doing well? Which one(s) needs improvement?

_____
_____
_____
_____
_____
_____
_____
_____
_____
_____

On the continuum from contempt to tolerating to caring to genuine love, what are the challenges and payoffs of moving toward a flourishing marriage?

_____
_____
_____
_____
_____
_____
_____
_____
_____
_____

If you're married, are you willing to ask your spouse, "What would it look like for me to be attentive to your needs?" When and how will you enter this conversation and ask the question of your spouse?

_____
_____
_____
_____
_____
_____
_____
_____
_____
_____

What are some reasons it's important to understand that present marital frustrations are rooted in past lived experiences?

_____
_____
_____
_____
_____
_____
_____
_____
_____
_____

CHAPTER 11

Flourishing at Work

No job is a perfect fit. All work includes some drudgery, but it shouldn't be all drudgery.

READING TIME

As you read Chapter 11: "Flourishing at Work" in *The Flourishing Advantage*, review, reflect on, and respond to the text by answering the following questions.

REVIEW, REFLECT, AND RESPOND

Are you surprised at the Gallup survey report that the vast majority of people are passively engaged or actively disengaged at work? What do you think this points to?

_____
_____
_____
_____
_____
_____
_____
_____

How does the role of a manager or team leader impact team engagement according to Gallup's research, and what percentage of the variance in team engagement do they account for?

_____
_____
_____
_____
_____
_____
_____
_____
_____

What are the four levels of employee engagement outlined in this chapter, and how do they progress from basic needs to higher levels of fulfillment and commitment?

___

How would you state and explain the significance of your purpose in life?

___

According to Dave Kerpen, founder and CEO of Apprentice, what are the five reasons why purpose-driven companies thrive? Provide a brief explanation of each reason.

If you are actively engaged and fulfilled in your career, what childhood experiences or signs indicated that your current career path might be a good fit for you? How do your purposes at home and work align?

_____
_____
_____
_____
_____
_____
_____
_____
_____
_____
_____
_____
_____
_____
_____

For those who are passively disengaged or actively disengaged at work, what steps can be taken to identify a better career fit? How can self-reflection and seeking support from trusted individuals contribute to finding fulfillment in one's career?

_____
_____
_____
_____

Review the Key Questions and answer the ones that fit your attitude at work today.

CHAPTER 12

Unleash Your Potential!

*Flourishing begins with us, but
it doesn't end with us.*

READING TIME

As you read Chapter 12: "Unleash Your Potential!" in *The Flourishing Advantage*, review, reflect on, and respond to the text by answering the following questions.

REVIEW, REFLECT, AND RESPOND

How does the chapter illustrate the importance of embracing the present moment and focusing on future opportunities rather than dwelling on past achievements or failures?

_____
_____
_____
_____
_____
_____
_____
_____

Discuss the concept of resilience as presented in the chapter. How can individuals use their challenges and stressors as opportunities for growth and development?

_____
_____
_____
_____
_____
_____
_____
_____
_____

Explore the idea of prioritizing self-care for overall well-being. Why is it essential to attend to one's own needs alongside fulfilling responsibilities to others?

_____
_____
_____
_____
_____
_____
_____
_____
_____
_____
_____
_____

Reflect on the significance of maintaining a strengths-based perspective. How does recognizing and leveraging one's strengths contribute to a sense of empowerment and confidence?

_____
_____
_____
_____
_____
_____
_____
_____
_____
_____
_____
_____

Summarize the strategies outlined in the chapter for reframing stressful experiences and cultivating a positive mindset in the face of adversity.

_____
_____
_____
_____
_____
_____
_____
_____
_____
_____

Discuss the role of trusted relationships in fostering resilience and well-being.

_____
_____
_____
_____
_____
_____
_____
_____
_____
_____

Explore the notion of finding meaning and purpose in personal and professional roles. How can individuals align their actions with their values to lead fulfilling lives?

_____
_____
_____
_____
_____
_____
_____
_____
_____
_____

Discuss the role of creativity in navigating unexpected challenges and exploring innovative solutions. How can stepping out of one's comfort zone lead to personal and professional growth?

_____
_____
_____
_____
_____
_____
_____
_____
_____
_____

www.ingramcontent.com/pod-product-compliance
Lightning Source LLC
Chambersburg PA
CBHW062121080426
42734CB00012B/2942